CAMBRIDGE INTRODUCTION TO THE HISTORY OF MANKIND · TOPIC BOOK
GENERAL EDITOR · TREVOR CAIRNS

295

An Australian in the First World War

Bill Gammage

CAMBRIDGE UNIVERSITY PRESS
Cambridge
London · New York · Melbourne

To Mum and Dad

Published by the Syndics of the Cambridge University Press
The Pitt Building, Trumpington Street, Cambridge CB2 1RP
Bentley House, 200 Euston Road, London NW1 2DB
32 East 57th Street, New York, NY 10022, USA
296 Beaconsfield Parade, Middle Park, Melbourne 3206, Australia

First published 1976

Printed in Great Britain by
W. S. Cowell Ltd, Butter Market, Ipswich

Library of Congress cataloguing in publication data
Gammage, Bill.
An Australian in the First World War.
(Cambridge introduction to the history of mankind: Topic book)
SUMMARY: Presents an account of the part played by the Australian army in the First World War by following a 'typical' soldier from training to trenches.
1. European War, 1914–1918 – Australia – Juvenile literature. 2. Australia – History – 20th century – Juv. lit. 3. European War, 1914–1918 – Campaigns – juv. lit. [1. European War, 1914–1918 – Australia. 2. Australia – History – 20th century. 3. European War, 1914–1918 – Campaigns]
I. Title.
D547.A8G33   940.4'09'94   76–111
ISBN 0 521 21018 6

Drawings by David Harris and Mike Cole
Maps by Reg Piggott

cover: *Australians attacking Lone Pine, Gallipoli, 6 August 1915. The Australian War Memorial model shows the Turkish front trenches covered with heavy pine logs (see page 20).*

Acknowledgements

My chief thanks are to the thousand men, both living and dead, of the First A.I.F., whose diaries and letters and advice provided the information for this story. Most of their records, and almost all the photographs reproduced here, are in the Library of the Australian War Memorial, Canberra, and I thank my friends there for their help and kindness over several years. My wife Jan typed the manuscript, Mr Les Gumley, Mr N. L. Joyner, and Mrs M. L. Rossiter have given me advice or permission to use photographs, and the series editor and staff of Cambridge University Press have worked hard to make my manuscript presentable to readers. I am grateful to them all.

Illustrations appear by kind permission of the following: cover, pp. 3, 4, 5, 9, 11(below), 12, 13, 14, 15, 16, 17, 18, 19(men swimming), 20, 22, 23, 24, 25, 27, 28, 30, 32, 33, 34, 35, 36, 37, 38, 39, 40, 41, 43, 44(top), 45, 46, 48 Australian War Memorial; p. 11(top) Mrs M. L. Rossiter; pp. 19, 35 Imperial War Museum; p. 26 Cambridge University Library, Times Newspapers Ltd and *The Guardian*.

You can learn more about the First World War by looking at the *Official History of Australia in the War of 1914–18* by C. E. W. Bean. It has twelve volumes, including one volume of photographs. Dr Bean has also written a shorter history of the war, called *Anzac to Amiens*.

Contents

How we learn about the Great War

Much has been written about the First World War, either by soldiers or statesmen who took part in it, or by historians later, trying to describe what it was like or why it began. The books, papers, notes, articles, maps and photographs that these people have left are very valuable in helping us to learn about the war.

This story, however, is not about the war as a whole, but about one ordinary soldier in one army which fought in the war. 'Tom' is an imaginary soldier. He did not really exist. But the things he and his friends said or did were actually said or done by ordinary Australian soldiers during the war.

How do we know this? Books and articles help us a little, but the most useful information comes from diaries or letters that ordinary Australian soldiers wrote during the war, or from talking to Australian soldiers who fought in the war and are still alive.

In the Australian War Memorial in Canberra there is a large collection of wartime diaries and letters written by Australian soldiers. All the incidents described in this story (and often the words used in the description) are recorded somewhere in that War Memorial collection. Most of the incidents described here did actually happen to men of the 3rd Battalion, the battalion to which the imaginary soldier in our story belongs.

This story has also been shown to Australians who fought in the Great War (as it was then called), to see whether it really describes the war as they remember it. In this way we know that even the words the soldiers speak in this story are words used by Australian soldiers at the time, even though sometimes these words may seem strange to us.

Although this is a story, then, it is also an attempt to write accurate history – to tell you what it was like to be an Australian in the First World War.

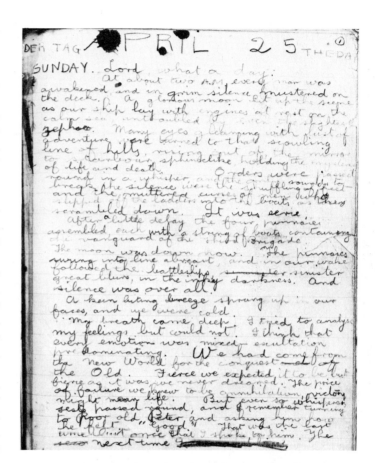

An extract from the diary of an Australian corporal, George Mitchell, describing the landing at Anzac.

left: *Painting of 'The Beach at Anzac' by Frank Crozier.*

1 Why the war began

Europe in 1914

Entente Powers 1914
Allies of the Entente Powers
Neutral States 1914
Central Powers 1914
Allies of the Central Powers but remaining neutral August 1914

The Great War began on 1 August 1914 and ended on 11 November 1918. It was fought between the Entente Powers (later called the Allies), led by the British Empire, France and Russia, and the Central Powers, led by Germany, Austria–Hungary and Turkey. If you look at the two maps you can see that many of these nations were much larger in 1914 than they were by 1920.

Before the war these nations had been rivals. Their peoples believed that their safety depended on being stronger than their neighbours, and that power and prestige were admirable and worthwhile things for a nation to have. So they competed in trade and commerce, they built large armies and navies, and spoke of how glorious their nation was, how much better it was than any other.

Yet the nations of Europe also feared each other. They were afraid that other nations might combine against them, or that by a sudden attack a neighbour might overwhelm their defences, just as Germany had overrun France in a war in 1871. To protect themselves against such possibilities the nations did two main things.

Firstly, their armies and navies made plans for what they should do if war did begin. All the armies were to be ready to attack *quickly* if war broke out, because the generals believed that whichever country was able to attack first would have the best chance of winning. We can see now that these plans were really very risky, because they meant that as soon as one nation began to organize its armies for war, or 'mobilize', all the other nations would prepare for war by mobilizing too, to make sure

Europe in 1920

they were not attacked before their armies were quite ready.

Secondly, the great nations of Europe looked for allies, to help them if they became involved in war. Germany and Austria-Hungary had been close friends since 1879, and by 1907 Britain, France and Russia became friends. By 1914 Europe was split into two camps, each suspicious and fearful of the other. This was a dangerous situation, because if any nation mobilized, the network of European plans and alliances could spring into use, and sweep the nations one after another into war.

That is exactly what happened in 1914. On 28 June Archduke Franz Ferdinand, of the royal house of Austria-Hungary, was shot dead by Serbian nationalists at Sarajevo, in the Balkans. Austria-Hungary mobilized against Serbia, so Serbia's ally, Russia, mobilized against Austria-Hungary. When this happened Austria-Hungary's ally, Germany, was obliged by her military plans to mobilize against Russia and against Russia's ally, France. When Germany invaded neutral Belgium, Britain came into the war on 4 August, and so within six weeks the shooting of one man in the Balkans had tumbled almost all of Europe into war. No nation imagined how long that war would last, or how terrible it would be.

2 Australia enters the war

Australia entered the war because it was part of the British Empire. In 1914 almost all Australians called themselves 'British'. They were proud of their British heritage, and anxious to prove themselves worthy members of the British Empire. Even before England declared war on Germany, Australia was eager to help the Mother Country, and almost every Australian agreed with the leader of the Labor Party, Andrew Fisher, who declared that if war came, Australia would support England 'to the last man and the last shilling'.

When war did come, Australians greeted it with an enthusiasm unparalleled in their history. Cheering crowds filled the streets, thousands of men rushed to join the army, and thousands of pounds were offered to help the war effort. A few people opposed the war, but generally the Australian government had so many offers of help that it could not possibly have accepted them all.

Why were Australians so ready to fight? We must remember that the peoples of many countries were eager for war in 1914 because they thought war was a manly and admirable thing. Australia herself had never fought in a big war, yet Australians shared with other Europeans this belief that success in a major war was the best test of whether a nation was healthy and

The First Australian Division in 1914

	NEW SOUTH WALES	VICTORIA	OUTER STATES	TOTAL
INFANTRY	*First Brigade* 1st, 2nd, 3rd, 4th Battalions 4,080 men HQ 50 men	*Second Brigade* 5th, 6th, 7th, 8th Battalions 4,080 men HQ 50 men	*Third Brigade* 9th (Qld), 10th (SA), 11th (SA, WA), 12th (Tas, WA, SA) Battalions 4,080 men HQ 50 men	12,390
MEDICAL CORPS *attached to infantry*	*1st Field Ambulance* 230 men	*2nd Field Ambulance* 230 men	*3rd Field Ambulance* 230 men	690
ENGINEERS *attached to infantry*	*1st Field Company* 220 men	*2nd Field Company* 220 men	*3rd Field Company* 220 men	660
ARTILLERY	*First Field Brigade* 1st, 2nd, 3rd Batteries 600 men HQ 20 men Brigade Ammunition Column 100 men	*Second Field Brigade* 4th, 5th, 6th Batteries 600 men HQ 20 men Brigade Ammunition Column 100 men	*Third Field Brigade* 7th, 8th, 9th Batteries 600 men HQ 20 men Brigade Ammunition Column 100 men	2,160
LIGHT HORSE	*First Light Horse Brigade* 1st (NSW), 2nd (Qld), 3rd (SA, Tas) Regts 1,650 men	4th (Vic) Regt, Divisional troops 550 men	HQ 30 men Brigade troops 150 men 1st Light Horse Field Ambulance 120 men	2,500
Infantry Divisional Headquarters 200 men	*Infantry Auxiliary Divisional Troops* 280 men		*Artillery Divisional Ammunition Column* 120 men	600
				19,000

(Key: *Qld* = Queensland; *NSW* = New South Wales; *Tas* = Tasmania; *Vic* = Victoria; *SA* = South Australia; *WA* = West Australia)

Australians off to the war, September 1914.

vigorous. Britain had won a whole Empire by war, and this seemed to prove her strength – so Australians wanted to show that they too could pass the test of battle. In addition, Australians imagined that they had particular reasons for wanting to fight. They expected the British Empire to protect them if their country were ever attacked, so the First World War gave them an opportunity to help Britain in turn.

Later in the war, many Australians became less eager to fight. The war became too terrible for it to be seen as a glorious event, and when this happened Australians kept fighting only because they considered it their duty. In this period Australians supported the war because they thought German methods of war and government barbaric and undemocratic.

As soon as the war began, Australia set about raising the army it would send overseas to fight. It was called the Australian Imperial Force, or A.I.F., a name which neatly balanced Australian attitudes towards their country and their Empire. In 1914 it was proposed to recruit 20,000 soldiers into the A.I.F., but by 1918 over 416,000 men had enlisted, and more than 330,000 of them had sailed overseas to fight.

Most Australian soldiers were infantry, and by 1916 there were five infantry divisions in the A.I.F. Each division contained twelve battalions – in other words, there were sixty infantry battalions in the A.I.F. by 1916. At full strength a battalion contained about 1,000 men, and his battalion became a soldier's home: to it his mail and his other links with home were directed, and with it he lived, trained, fought and died.

Our story is mainly about a man in the 3rd Battalion, Tom Mitchell, and when we begin he has already sailed overseas. He is sitting with some of his mates outside a tent in the vast, sprawling A.I.F. camp at Mena, under the shadow of the ancient pyramids of Egypt. It is early in April 1915.

3 The A.I.F. in Egypt

Tom Mitchell sat back against his tentpole and looked glumly across the sands of the Egyptian desert towards the pyramids.

'Crikey, it's hot!' he exclaimed. 'Nothing but heat and sand, sand, everlasting sand. At least at home we could find something to do when it got hot! Here all we do is *sit*, day after day, and put up with it. I'm sorry I joined the blasted army!'

'You should have thought of that before you volunteered,' his mate, Jack Sloane, told him, but everyone in the tent agreed with Tom. They had all volunteered to fight in the war – some for the tremendous adventure it would be, some to help the Empire, some to defend Australia, others simply because the pay was good (6 shillings a day), or because they had no jobs. But every man was keen to fight and had rushed to enlist in August or September 1914, eager to have a crack at the enemy.

They had landed in Egypt in December to help protect it from a Turkish invasion, and since then they had been camped in the hot desert, marching and training through sand and flies, eating sand in their food, exhausted by the heat, bored with the monotony of it all. There was not even a good pub! Everyone was utterly sick of Egypt, and wanted only to go somewhere, anywhere, to fight the enemy.

Just as Tom was suggesting to Jack that they climb the pyramids for the tenth time, Paddy Halliday, the sergeant, came along. 'All right you blokes, get your kits together,' he said. 'It looks as though we're off this time.'

'Really, Paddy?' Tom asked.

'Too right! Tonight. And we're going to fight!'

'You beauty!' Tom yelled, and he and Jack leapt across the

The A.I.F. camp at Mena, February 1915.

below: *Men of the First Division training in Egypt.*

sand, laughing and joking, and joyfully calling out the news to soldiers passing by. Soon cheering began, first here, then there, finally swelling and roaring until the whole camp was shouting and singing, filled with elation at the exciting prospect before them.

'I wonder where we're going?' Tom asked.

'France – the Western Front – to fight the Germans', Jack answered.

'No, they wouldn't have kept us in Egypt so long if we were going to France,' another soldier, Lofty Smith, broke in. 'I reckon we're going to the Dardanelles, to fight the Turks.'

'The Turks aren't as dangerous as the Germans,' Jack said.

'But if we leave them alone they can attack Egypt, and besides, England can't send supplies to Russia while Turkey controls the Dardanelles. What do you reckon, Andy?' Lofty turned to ask Andrew Ellis, their corporal.

Now Tom, Jack and Lofty were all bushmen. Tom and Jack had enlisted together from the plains of the Riverina in western New South Wales; Lofty came from the hills of the Monaro, near the Snowy Mountains in southern New South Wales. About a lot of things, such as riding, shooting, or living off the land, they knew much more than Andy, who had been a school-teacher in Sydney before he joined the A.I.F. But Andy was quiet and efficient, he had been in the peacetime militia before the war, and he had a brother who was an officer in another battalion, so on matters of military strategy his opinion was much respected.

'I think the whole First Division is off to the Dardanelles,' Andy replied, 'to somewhere near where the British Navy tried to break through to Constantinople last month.'

11

The 2nd and 3rd Battalions practising for the Anzac landing, Lemnos, April 1915.

That seemed to settle it, and most Australian soldiers agreed that they were going to fight the Turk.

By evening the men of the 3rd Battalion had packed their battle kits, written hasty letters home to Australia, struck their tents and marched into Cairo. There they saw their leaders – General Bridges, who commanded the First Australian Division, and General Birdwood, who commanded all the Australians and New Zealanders who had come to fight in the war. The Australians and New Zealanders had been formed into a body called the Australian and New Zealand Army Corps, and already men were beginning to call it the Anzac Corps.

From Cairo the 3rd Battalion went by train to the docks at Alexandria. By morning the men were at sea, sailing northwards, and watching anxiously for enemy submarines. But they arrived safely off Lemnos Island in the Aegean Sea, and dropped anchor in the bay. As Tom looked over the island he could see soldiers everywhere, Australians, New Zealanders, British and Frenchmen, all united in the common cause, all undergoing their final training for the approaching battle. Men were climbing from the ships into small boats, rowing furiously to land and charging ashore, marching up hills, marching down again and re-embarking onto the landing boats, rowing back out to the ships, and then going through the whole exercise again. For three weeks this intense training was kept up, and the soldiers worked willingly, because they knew that soon they would be in action.

At last, at dusk on 24 April 1915, Tom saw the ships of the Allies putting to sea, sliding away from Lemnos and rounding towards the east. A little while later their officer called them together and lined them on parade, Paddy Halliday, Andy Ellis, Tom, Jack, Lofty and the others. Their officer was Lieutenant Ross, a Scotsman who had served in the British Army before he came to Australia, and he told them quietly that they were bound for the Gallipoli Peninsula, beside the Dardanelles. On the following day, 25 April 1915, they were to take part in

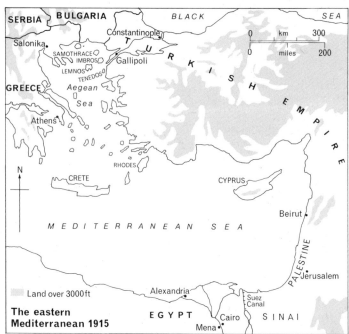

The eastern Mediterranean 1915

Land over 3000 ft

the largest seaborne landing in British history. The Australians and New Zealanders, the Anzacs, were to land separately from the rest of the army. They were to capture a strip of land across the peninsula, so that the ships of the British Navy could later sail up the narrow waters and attack the Turkish capital, Constantinople. They would land at dawn. That landing would be their chance to show both their own country and the rest of the world how Australians could fight.

4 The landing at Anzac

Softly the line of ships crept toward the Turks. The British and French troops were to land at Cape Helles, at the tip of the Gallipoli Peninsula, and at Kum Kale, across the water nearby. The Anzacs were bound for Gaba Tepe, further up the peninsula. The first Australians to land would be the Third Brigade, and their ships were far ahead of Tom's boat, steaming through the night. The Third Brigade would land at dawn, and as the momentous hour approached, Tom and his mates stood straining to catch the first sound of firing.

At 4.29 a.m., echoing faintly over the quiet water, the first shot came. Another followed, then two more, until finally there arose a crescendo of noise as the Turks roused themselves and began firing on the boats advancing to meet them.

'They've landed!' Tom shouted, and cheer after cheer rang round the transport, for no one doubted that the soldiers of the Third would succeed. Tom and his friends eagerly crowded the ship's rail to catch their first glimpse of the battlefield, and soon they saw it before them: steep, grey cliffs rising from the water's edge, and across the skyline above, figures moving, as calmly as though walking to the bus stop. There was no mistaking that casual gait: the men were Australians. The Third Brigade was ashore.

Now it was the 3rd Battalion's turn. As the men climbed into their landing boats Tom could hear the plop! plop! plop! of bullets striking the sea around them. Quickly the soldiers rowed for the shore, laughing and talking excitedly, confidently predicting victory in the coming battle.

Suddenly Lofty Smith let out a yell. 'By crikey! I'm hit!' he roared. 'Oh, the rotten dogs! They've shot me before I've had a chance to take a crack at them! Oh crikey!'

'Shut up and let me look,' said Andy Ellis. 'Huh! Just as I thought, it's only a scratch. You wouldn't be yelling like that if you were really hurt. You'll be all right.' So Lofty sat down and bandaged his wound, and muttered that that was just what you would expect a school-teacher to say!

Australians drawn up on the deck of a battleship on the eve of the landing at Anzac.

below: *Heading for the shore, Anzac, 25 April 1915.*

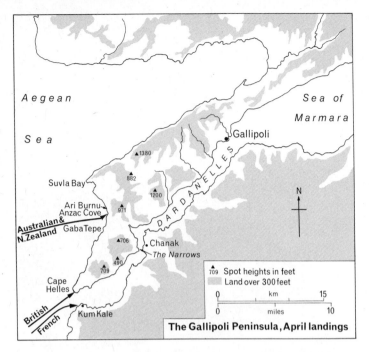

The Gallipoli Peninsula, April landings

The boats touched land, and the men jumped out and splashed ashore. They were not at Gaba Tepe – that lay about 3 kilometres to the south. Instead they were near a point which the Turks called Ari Burnu, and everywhere in front of them lay steep hills covered with small prickly bushes. They stood on a little pebble-strewn beach, for which the Turks had no name because it was so insignificant, but which soon all the world would know as Anzac Cove.

From the hills came a constant trickle of wounded Australians, sometimes bringing a prisoner or two with them, and already the beach was filling with men waiting to be taken to the hospital ships. Here and there Australian dead lay scattered, men of the Third Brigade shot as they landed; near Tom a young engineer lay crumpled by the edge of the water, the bright red bloodstain on his back slowly turning black.

There was little time to think about such things. The Turks were counter-attacking. Their shrapnel was bursting over the beach, and up on the ridges the Australian line was being hard pressed.

'Come on, 3rd Battalion, follow me!' cried Lieutenant Ross, and in single file they followed him inland, up a steep narrow valley towards the enemy. Soon they came upon an officer, tired and dirty, who greeted them wearily.

'Thank heavens! You must hurry. The Turks are pushing us everywhere. The men are holding on, but they're short of ammunition and water, and they need help. Go and strengthen the line at the head of this gully, and hurry!'

Lieutenant Ross rushed his men up the gully. They climbed steeply, sometimes on hands and knees, but quickly they reached the top, and there found a thin line of men lying along the edge of the crest. They were mainly West Australians, from the 11th Battalion: several were dead, most were wounded, and only a few could still fire at the enemy. They were hot, thirsty and weary. Bullets came at them from both front and rear, for many Turks still lay in the scrub behind the Australians, shooting them down. Every officer was dead, but the men still wanted to fight, and they were determined not to let the Turks beat them. Lieutenant Ross took them under his command, and reinforced their line with the soldiers of the 3rd.

'Jesus, this is dangerous!' exclaimed Lofty, as the bullets whizzed past. 'The army ought to look after us better than this, or we'll want compensation.' The others laughed, but then Jack Sloane shouted, 'Here they come!' Through the scrub Tom could see the dull green uniforms of the Turks as they ran forward. Every Australian rifle was turned upon them, and the front rang with fire, until at last the Turks gave up their attack, and disappeared back into the scrub.

Almost at once a message came, ordering the men to go forward. Lieutenant Ross decided to advance about 50 metres to the far side of the ridge, where he thought the Australians might shoot more easily at their enemies. He sprang to his feet, calling 'Come on, Australia! Charge!' but as he uttered the words a Turkish bullet hit him in the chest, and he fell quietly backward, and lay still. His men ran forward, following Sergeant Halliday, and soon the Turks opened their full fire upon them. Rifles, machine-guns and shrapnel shells clattered and roared, and bullets swept the Australians from every direction. Man after man fell, but still the line went on gallantly, until at last the survivors flung themselves gasping along the far side of the ridge, and began to dig for their lives for shelter.

Tom looked about him. The position seemed hopeless. One bullet had gone through his hat, another through the heel of his boot, a third through his water bottle, and two more through his tunic. Jack Sloane had been shot in the hand, Andy Ellis and Lofty Smith were nowhere to be seen. The survivors were pressing themselves grimly into the earth, hoping not to be hit. Bullets flew from all directions, shrapnel burst regularly, and every now and then an Australian would give a low cry as he was struck.

'What can we do, Paddy?' Tom asked his sergeant.

'I don't know,' Paddy replied. 'We can't go forward there aren't enough of us left. And we can't go back – we'd all be shot. We'll just have to stay where we are till it gets dark.'

So throughout that long afternoon the small band of Australians lay huddled along the ridge, and all over the battlefield similar groups lay, some Anzac, some Turkish, every man fighting bravely to defend or capture some ridge or gully, because each metre seemed vital.

Night fell, and Tom, Paddy, Jack and the others crept back across the ridge, bringing their wounded with them as gently as they could, and at last dropping thankfully behind the crest from which they had charged so gallantly that afternoon.

There sat Lofty Smith, almost exactly where he had been before the advance began.

'What are you doing here, Lofty?' Tom asked, surprised.

'Oh well,' said Lofty, 'I've seen enough of the war, so I thought I'd go back to Australia.' He pointed to his foot. A Turkish sniper, firing from somewhere behind, had shot it away.

'Andy's dead,' added Lofty quietly. 'He's out in No Man's Land.'

There was a moment's silence, then Jack and three other wounded men lifted Lofty up, and trudged slowly off towards the beach and the hospital ship. The rest bent wearily, and all that night dug a trench to protect them when morning came. Towards dawn they found the body of their lieutenant, went down the valley a little, dug a shallow grave, and laid their comrade to rest. Then they climbed back to the trenches and, utterly exhausted, slept.

5 Gallipoli

'What fools we are!' Tom Mitchell declared. 'Remember how eager we were to fight? Remember how the people cheered in Sydney, and the girls kissed us and cried over us when we left? Remember how bored we were in Egypt? I wish I was back in Egypt now! Or better still, back in Australia, with the war won. I'll never leave Australia again after I get back.'

It was ten days after that famous Sunday of the landing at Anzac. Tom and the others had fought on the ridge for three days, and soon where they had fought would become known as the Bloody Angle, because of the number of men who died there. Since the landing, over a third of the battalion had been killed or wounded, and almost all the survivors were dirty, weary and dispirited, for modern war had proved to be nothing like the glorious adventure they had imagined it would be.

Nonetheless, the survivors of the landing felt that they had gone through a very special experience, not only because they personally had passed a difficult test, but also because they felt that what they had done had helped make Australia and New Zealand nations. Their deeds had won the respect of the world, and almost at a stroke had raised their countries from dependencies to a seat at the table of nations. Few ordinary men in history had given any country so much, and they knew it, and were proud of it.

Also, it seemed to observers that a strong fraternity had grown up among them. Their mateship had acquired a special quality, that of having together faced and survived the great challenge of death, and of having together to face it in future. Thereafter, throughout the war, the willingness to help a mate became an important part of the creed of Australian and New Zealand soldiers.

And the Anzacs had not been beaten. They held a strong line of trenches, and they were determined that the Turks would never drive them away. The war was no longer glorious or exciting, but it was still necessary, and the Anzacs remained convinced that they fought for a just cause and the honour of their King and Country. If their generals wanted them to fight, they were ready.

Between April and June 1915 several terrible battles were fought on Gallipoli, at Courtney's Post, at Steele's Post, at German Officer's Trench, at the Knife Edge, and above all at Quinn's Post. The narrow ridge at Quinn's overlooked almost the entire Anzac position, so both sides fought desperately to capture it. Regularly the lines at Quinn's would burst into furious bomb (grenade) and bayonet fights which almost annihilated both garrisons. But fresh troops took their places, and for week after week the savage slaughter continued. At length, in June, both sides abandoned the struggle at Quinn's, and became content with the ground they held.

15th Battalion soldiers waiting to counter-attack at Quinn's.

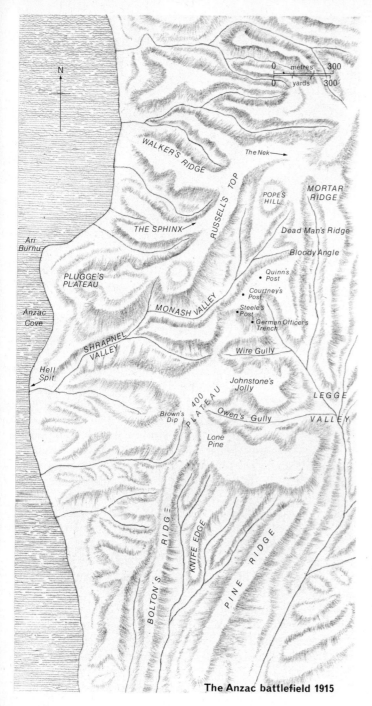

The Anzac battlefield 1915

left: *A sniper at Anzac.*

below: *A reserve trench on Anzac.*

The men of the 3rd Battalion took little part in these trench battles. They manned comparatively 'quiet' sectors of the front line, and passed most of their time digging their trenches deeper and making them more comfortable, watching for Turks to snipe, scavenging behind the lines for firewood, carrying food, water and ammunition up from the beaches to the trenches,

Making bombs (hand grenades) from old jam tins, Anzac.

below: Soldiers on water fatigue, Anzac.

and, at night, crawling out into No Man's Land to erect barbed wire defences or to see what the Turks were doing.

It was boring work usually, and flies in millions brought much sickness; there was not enough water, and too many lice, and too little mail from home. Perhaps worst of all the food was poor: it was mainly tinned bully beef, although Tom declared that a bull would not recognize it, and biscuits, which were so hard that Paddy Halliday offered a prize to the first man who could eat three without breaking a tooth! Usually the soldiers had tea, sometimes apricot jam – and there was another prize for the man who actually found a piece of apricot in it – and occasionally men could buy chocolate and condensed milk from the beach canteen. Once or twice a lucky man would get a parcel of tinned fruit or cake or toffees from Australia, and then all his friends would gather, and within half an hour the parcel would vanish!

One clear hot day, after they had been digging trenches on Johnston's Jolly, Paddy Halliday took his men down to the beach for a swim. They arrived to find the sea full of soldiers, swimming and splashing gaily, ignoring the shrapnel which the Turkish artillery every now and then burst over the beach.

left: *Men swimming on North Beach, Anzac.*

below: *Weapons used by the Australians on Anzac.*

A Vickers medium
machine-gun.

A short magazine Lee
Enfield Mark 3 rifle.

'Hope there's no sharks about,' a man called to Tom as a shell burst close by. 'Come on in, the water's fine!' So Tom and Paddy and the others splashed in, and for an hour had a glorious time in the water. Then they dressed, filled kerosene tins with fresh water brought from the ships in the bay, and climbed back to their trenches.

On Johnston's Jolly the 3rd Battalion was buzzing with excitement.

'Have you heard? We're going to attack Lone Pine!' a man called.

'Crikey, are we? When?' answered Tom.

'I don't know, but tonight the Second Brigade is coming up to relieve us, and we're going behind the lines to get ready. The whole of the First Brigade will be attacking.'

Tom and his friends were eager to attack. They hoped the assault on Lone Pine, part of a general British offensive on Gallipoli, would help win the war, and besides they were tired of sitting in the trenches. Willingly they prepared for battle – cleaning their rifles, sharpening their bayonets, filling their water bottles, writing letters home, sewing white calico patches on their backs and sleeves so that they could tell friend from foe when they got to the Turkish trenches, and stacking in a safe place the kit they would not need during the battle.

Just then some reinforcements arrived, fresh from Egypt. One came up to Tom.

'Excuse me, are you Tom Mitchell?' he asked.

'That's right.'

'I'm Mick Sloane, Jack's younger brother. He told me to look out for the ugliest man in the battalion, and I'd find you.'

Tom smiled. 'Well, that would be right, now he's away. How is he?'

'Oh, he's all right,' Mick answered. 'He'll be back here in a couple of months. I say, is it true we're going to make an attack this afternoon? That's bonzer! I can't wait to get started!' His eyes sparkled with excitement.

'Huh! You won't think that after you've been through it,' Tom replied. 'You'd better stick close to me, or to Paddy Halliday, that sergeant over there. He's another mate of Jack's. Have you got a cobber?'

'Yes,' Mick answered. 'Hey Rodney!' He turned back to Tom. 'Rodney has never been out of his office in Sydney in his life, so I have to look after him a bit.' Rodney came over, smiled awkwardly and said hello, and then while Tom made both the new arrivals a cup of tea they agreed to stick together during the coming battle.

By late that afternoon the First Brigade was in the trenches waiting to attack. A line of men crouched along the firestep of the trench (on the right in the above photo), ready to spring forward when the attack whistles blew. Two other lines stood ready to follow them, and overhead the British artillery roared, so loudly that the men could not hear themselves speak. Suddenly the shellfire stopped, there was a moment's silence, then up and down the line the whistles shrilled.

'Right, over we go!' shouted Tom, and the line of Australians plunged forward, sprinting across the wide bare plateau towards the Turkish trenches.

Here and there a Turkish rifle began to flash, then more as the Turks realized what was happening, then a machine-gun, then two, until soon the air was full of the familiar sounds of bullets whipping and cracking as they passed close by.

The Australians ran on, and after 80 metres they came to the front Turkish trench. It was covered with heavy pine logs, seemingly impenetrable! The attackers halted for a moment, puzzled. Then some ran on into the Turkish rear trenches, while others began tearing at the logs, levering them away, and dropping into the darkness beneath.

Tom, Mick and Rodney found a gap in the Turkish head

cover and ran down into the enemy's trench. Almost immediately a shot came from the darkness, and Mick felt a hard blow in his thigh.

'Cripes, this is getting serious!' he exclaimed as his leg collapsed beneath him, and he fell down against the side of the trench. Three Turks ran forward, and Tom and Rodney turned to face them. Bayonet clashed on bayonet, thrust, parry, thrust again. A Turk jabbed his bayonet at Tom's throat, but Tom knocked it aside; the Turk overbalanced and tripped forward, and Tom bayonetted him in the stomach. Mick fired, and a

second Turk fell. Rodney let out a cry of pain as the third Turk thrust a bayonet into his arm, then ran back along the trench and skipped safely round a corner. More Australians jumped into the trench, and soon it was in Australian hands.

Tom looked at Mick's wound. It was losing a lot of blood, and already Mick's face was turning white. Tom staunched the flow.

'There,' he exclaimed, 'that will do you for a little while, but you need to get to an aid post quickly. I can't go, and – ' he stood up to look at the shells and bullets sweeping across No

Man's Land – 'I don't think anyone will be able to come and get you.' A worried frown wrinkled his brow.

Without a word Rodney stepped forward, hoisted Mick onto his shoulder, and walked back into No Man's Land. Bravely he went, bullets kicking around his feet, his mate on one shoulder, his wounded arm hanging limply from the other. Tom watched him go, then turned back to the fray.

For four days and nights, from 6 to 9 August, the battle raged at Lone Pine. Many times the Turks counter-attacked. Many times the Australians pushed them back, or attempted to advance themselves. Throughout the maze of trenches the roar of the bombs did not cease. A thousand sharp, brave con-

tests were fought, and the dead piled thickly, choking the trenches and fouling the air with their odour. Some of the cruellest hand fighting of the war took place at Lone Pine, but at length the Turks gave up their attacks, and left about half their trenches in the hands of their enemies. By then more than 2,000 Australians and over 6,000 Turks had been killed or wounded, and seven Australians, two of them killed in the battle, had won the Victoria Cross.

The 3rd Battalion came out of Lone Pine after three days' fighting. The men were haggard and exhausted. Many were wounded, all were reeling under the strain of their awful experiences. Tom and Paddy were as weary as any, and when they

Another captured trench at Lone Pine.

reached the safety of their own back trenches, they sank down and slept.

The next day, because so many of the 3rd had been killed or wounded, Paddy was promoted to lieutenant, and Tom to corporal. Tom learnt that Rodney had got Mick safely on board a hospital ship and was himself at the beach hospital, waiting to go. After eight months' training they had been less than an hour in battle before being evacuated.

A few days later Tom began to feel ill. His temperature rose, he felt dizzy and listless. At first he ignored these symptoms, but gradually they grew worse, and at last Paddy ordered him to report sick. Tom tried to protest, but Paddy dragged him to the aid post and stood him before the medical officer.

After a quick check the doctor exclaimed, 'Enteric! Its hospital for you, my boy. We lose more men from that fever than we do in battle. It's the flies and the exhaustion, that's the trouble. Do you think you can walk down to the beach? Off you go then!' He gave Tom a pink ticket, and slowly Tom went towards the beach while Paddy hastily gathered his mate's things together, then helped him down to the shore.

'Well, goodbye Tom. Give my regards to Egypt, and good luck!'

'Thanks Paddy. Goodbye, and good luck to you too. Sorry I can't stay and help.'

Paddy turned back to the trenches, and by evening Tom was on the hospital ship. As it got under way he looked back across the darkening sea towards the steep sombre cliffs of Anzac, and wondered whether he would see them, or Paddy, or any of his friends, again.

23

6 The Australians arrive in France

It was October 1915. Tom lay weak and ill in hospital in Egypt. Jack and Rodney came regularly to see him: their wounds were healing rapidly, and Jack was almost ready to go back to Gallipoli. Lofty had been sent home to Australia, but Mick's wound was still serious, and he was under special care in a hospital on Lemnos.

The news from Gallipoli was bad. The August offensive of which Lone Pine was part had failed. Many soldiers had been killed, and the survivors were beginning to despair of ever winning the war.

But other stories came back, mostly about the Turks. Both Anzac and Turk had learnt to admire each other, and after August 1915 they frequently made contact across the trenches.

'Hey Turk,' an Australian would call, 'how far is it to Constantinople?'

And a voice would come back, 'How long will you take to get there? You haven't got far yet!'

Sometimes the Turks would throw over a bunch of onions, their main ration, and the Anzacs would throw back tins of bully beef, and then both sides would stew up bully beef and onions! Although the deadly game of war went on, a friendly rivalry grew between the trenches, and sixty years later old

Patients and nurses in a hospital in Egypt, 1915.

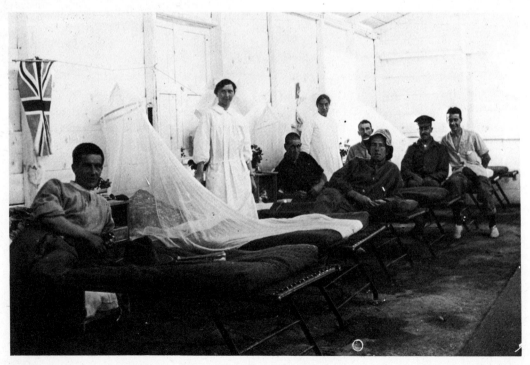

above: *In an A.I.F. hospital at Hurdcott, England.*

left: *Australian light horsemen.*

soldiers on both sides still spoke with admiration of their former enemies.

The man who usually brought the Gallipoli news into Tom's ward was a big, cheerful light horseman from Queensland, wounded during the August fighting on Anzac, and now helping the nurses with light duties around the wards while he recovered. The Light Horse had volunteered to leave their horses in Egypt and go to Gallipoli as infantry, and soon some of them were saying that it was the silliest thing they ever did. But now the big light horseman came with some special news for Tom.

'Well corporal,' he said, 'you're off to hospital in England. What do you think of that?'

England! Tom had never been there, but it was the heart of the Empire, and at school he had been taught many stories of the motherland. Already he could imagine the snow at Christmas, the narrow winding lanes, the grass always green, the cities crowded with people.

'Well, that sounds all right,' said Tom. 'I was beginning to think I'd never get there. When am I going?'

'Don't know,' answered the light horseman, 'but soon!'

He was right. Within a fortnight Tom had said goodbye to his mates, and was on the blue Mediterranean. A week later he watched the grey coastline of England rising slowly from the morning mists as they docked at Southampton, and before long he was safely in a convalescent hospital near Sutton Veny, a small village on Salisbury Plain in the south of England.

SUVLA AND ANZAC EVACUATED.

TURKS TAKEN BY SURPRISE.

SLIGHT CASUALTIES.

SUCCESSFUL COMBINED OPERATION.

The War Office makes the following announcement :—

All the troops at Suvla and Anzac, together with their guns and stores, have been successfully transferred with insignificant casualties to another sphere of operations.

The following further announcement was made by the War Office last evening :—

Some further details of the evacuation of Anzac and Suvla have been received.

Without the Turks being aware of the movement a great army has been withdrawn from one of the areas occupied on the Gallipoli Peninsula, although in closest contact with the enemy.

By this contraction of front operations at other points of the line will be more effectively carried out.

Two different reactions to the evacuation of Anzac. On the left, the War Office hails the evacuation as a complete success; on the right, the Manchester Guardian of 21 December 1915 argues that evacuation means defeat in the Gallipoli campaign, and attacks the bad leadership which led to the failure.

strategically, ... most wort... ...ing. When all is said that can be said against the Dardanelles enterprise, the fact remains that our going there was the first instance in which we wrested the strategical initiative from the enemy, and that had the enterprise been carried through to victory, as it very nearly was, we should have been appreciably nearer to the end of the war. The chance which in April and May was brilliant paled, however, as the year advanced and nothing decisive was done, and after the defeat at Suvla Bay disappeared altogether. To the disappearance of our hopes also contributed a number of mistakes in the field of which we have as yet had no official information. When all allowance has been made, we ought to have won at Suvla, and would have won with better management. It is due to those who have fought so well that all mistakes and all failures in professional duty should be relentlessly exposed. There is no desire to make victims, but no nation can do itself justice in a war unless victory is rewarded as it deserves. And neither valour nor virtue can be properly rewarded unless incompetence and mismanagement are exhibited side by side with them.

In the hospital Tom gradually recovered, and by Christmas he felt well enough to walk over to the ancient ruins of Stonehenge, and to explore the quaint, quiet English villages nearby, so different from anything in Australia. Everything was new and interesting, and Tom often went exploring outside the hospital, dodging the military police looking for men without leave passes, and wandering as far as he could over the Salisbury countryside.

Only one piece of news saddened him. In December 1915 Anzac was evacuated. Tom thought bitterly of Turks occupying the ground for which so many Anzacs had died. He knew the Anzacs had not been defeated in battle but had been ordered to leave, and he and all the Australians blamed the incompetence of the British generals for their defeat. So did the English newspapers, and that was some consolation, but for months the evacuation of Anzac remained a severe blow to the morale of Australian soldiers.

In January 1916 Tom was given eight days' leave, and made his way to Scotland, where he found the home in which Lieutenant Ross had been born. He told the dead officer's parents how gallantly their son had fallen, and how much his comrades from far Australia admired him. Eagerly the old couple listened till he had finished, then thanked him and said he must come to stay whenever he had leave from the army.

Australians in slouch hats on leave in Trafalgar Square, London.

Tom did stay two or three days, and thought how kind the British people were to the Australians and other soldiers from overseas. Everywhere was friendship and hospitality, and the days of Tom's recovery passed quickly. Only two things discomforted him – the rules of the hospital, which he usually ignored, and the bitter cold of winter, which was more severe than anything he had experienced in Australia.

In April Tom left hospital for a training camp, and learnt that soon he would rejoin his battalion. He was ready. He was fit, and he knew that the A.I.F. was moving to fight in France. He was impatient to see his mates again, and to find out what war on the Western Front was like.

Australians on Birmingham railway station, England.

But the army's bureaucracy moved very slowly. The months dragged by, and still Tom waited in the training camp. 'This is an insult to a veteran soldier,' he fumed, and again and again he paraded before the camp's commanding officer, demanding to be sent back to his unit. Finally orders came, and thankfully Tom joined a draft of soldiers bound for France. He crossed from Dover to Le Havre, and then spent ten days in an A.I.F. training camp in France, marching, practising bayonet fighting, digging trenches, scrambling over walls, and doing lots of other things Tom thought were a waste of time for an old soldier. At night instructors gave lessons about the Western Front, on how dangerous the German machine-guns were, how heavy the artillery fire was, and how alert one had to be for trench raids by the enemy.

At last it was time for Tom to rejoin his battalion, and he made a long journey across northern France, by train, by truck and on foot, until one evening he marched into a small village near Amiens and found his battalion.

'Why, it's Tom!' cried a familiar voice, and Jack Sloane ran forward to greet him. 'How are you? Here, come and sit down. Hey Paddy, look who's arrived!'

Paddy came up, then Rodney, and many more of Tom's old friends; they shook his hand, asked him questions about England, cleared a space in a big barn for him, brought him clean straw to sleep on, and generally made him feel welcome. Tom was very happy.

There were many new faces in the battalion, men who had joined after Tom had left, and Paddy introduced him to some of them.

'Tom, this is Joe Thompson, from Sydney. And there is George Watts – he's a Pom, but a good bloke. They'll both be in your section.'

Tom shook hands, and then Paddy said, 'Well Tom, you picked a good time to arrive. So far the battalion has had a quiet time in France, but in two days we go into a big attack on the Somme.'

The Somme was the river around which the British had launched their great offensive on 1 July 1916, and soon the entire First Australian Division was to join the attack. A big battle was looming for the 3rd Battalion.

'Righto!' Tom said. 'Where will we attack?'

'Pozières.'

'Pozières. Never heard of it. Must be a little place.'

It was a little place. But within a few days everyone in Australia would know of it, and for the rest of their lives no one in the A.I.F. would ever forget it.

28

7 Pozières

Tom and his friends were advancing to attack Pozières. All around, and away to the horizon, a continual ripple of light broke the dark night as the British guns shelled the German positions. German guns were firing too, bombarding the advancing Australians so heavily at times that the men had to run one at a time across exposed places. Every now and then a soft 'plop' and a faint odour would announce the arrival of German gas shells, and the men would hastily pull on their gas masks, and grope their way on. Soon they were in No Man's Land, creeping closer and closer to the line of British shells bursting on the German trenches in front of them.

'If we can get close to our own barrage we won't have to run so far when it stops,' Paddy explained to Tom. 'This gives the Germans less time to come out of shelter and start shooting at us.'

Suddenly the British barrage stopped. The Australians sprinted forward and quickly reached the German front trench, but few Germans were there: most had been killed or were hiding from the British shellfire. Here and there a man raised his hands in surrender; occasionally a soldier stood bravely firing or throwing stick bombs for a few seconds before he was killed. At one point some Germans raced towards a machine-gun, but were shot as they got it working. The First Division swept forward, over the trench, and into the village beyond.

Pozières village no longer existed. Before the war it had been a small farming centre, with neat houses and green poplar trees lining the main road the Romans had built 2,000 years before. Now only a few stumps and a few ruined buildings remained. The Australians moved through these ruins, 'mopping up' stray Germans, and rolling phosphorous bombs into the cellars and dugouts and killing or capturing the garrison as it ran out. By morning Pozières was securely in A.I.F. hands, and individual Australians had begun searching for souvenirs to take home to Australia.

'Well, that wasn't too bad!' exclaimed Tom. 'Not many

The main street of Pozières, before the battle and after.

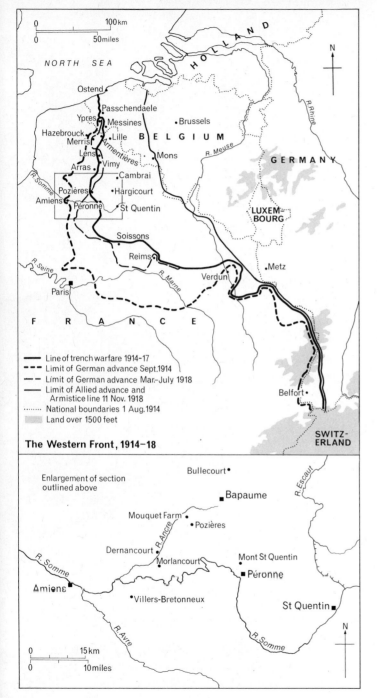

The Western Front, 1914–18

0 100 km
0 50 miles

NORTH SEA

HOLLAND

Ostend
Passchendaele
Ypres
Messines
• Brussels
Hazebrouck
Merris • Lille
Lens
Armentières
• Mons
Arras
Vimy
Cambrai
Pozières
• Hargicourt
Amiens
Péronne
• St Quentin

BELGIUM

R. Meuse

GERMANY

R. Rhine

LUXEM-
BOURG

Soissons

R. Somme

R. Seine

Reims

R. Marne

• Metz

Verdun

Paris

FRANCE

Belfort •

SWITZ-
ERLAND

—— Line of trench warfare 1914–17
- - - Limit of German advance Sept.1914
– – – Limit of German advance Mar.-July 1918
—— Limit of Allied advance and
      Armistice line 11 Nov. 1918
······ National boundaries 1 Aug.1914
      Land over 1500 feet

Enlargement of section
outlined above

Bullecourt •

■ Bapaume

R. Ancre

Mouquet Farm •
• Pozières

R. Escaut

R. Somme

Dernancourt •
Morlancourt •

Mont St Quentin •
■ Péronne

Amiens ■

• Villers-Bretonneux

R. Avre

St Quentin ■

R. Somme

0 15 km
0 10 miles

casualties, and we've had a great victory. If the war goes on like this, we'll soon be in Berlin!'

The others agreed, and everyone was pleased that the A.I.F. had done so well in its first big battle against German infantry.

But the Germans were determined to recapture Pozières, and soon a fierce artillery bombardment fell upon the Australian positions. Shells of every description rained down: high explosive which obliterated houses or killed twenty or thirty men in one terrible blast, shrapnel which sprayed small pellets of death for hundreds of metres in every direction, trench mortars which buried whole trenches of men alive, and gas, which blinded, or crept into the blood so that a day later soldiers suddenly began dropping dead. For six weeks, from 23 July to 3 September, the murderous fire continued. The green fields turned to brown, the small village was blasted so completely away that afterwards not even Frenchmen who had lived there could tell exactly where it had been. Even the hills changed their shape, and not one inch of the vast battlefield was left untouched by the German guns.

Under this merciless barrage the Australians lived and fought. Men were buried alive, dug out by their comrades, and buried again. Whole companies were destroyed, and some platoons which went into the barrage were never heard of again. The survivors huddled helplessly, praying that a shell would not land on them. Men went mad under the strain, and ran into the open, crying and shrieking. Some would suddenly start up and attack their friends, others would wander aimlessly, minds blank, for the cruel shells had destroyed their capacity to think. Never had Australian soldiers endured a more terrible bombardment.

By 27 July, only four days after it first attacked, the 3rd Battalion had lost almost five hundred men – more than half the battalion – and it was withdrawn. Tom hoped that he had seen the last of Pozières, but in the middle of August his battalion was again ordered into the line. The men feared to re-

31

Australians resting behind the line during the Pozières battle.

approach the dreaded shellfire, but they went, and soon once more were in the shattered line of holes and trenches that marked the Australian front.

'Now boys,' said Paddy Halliday, 'you see over there? That's Mouquet Farm, or what's left of it. Tonight we attack the German trenches in front of it. We won't start until after dark, but the 4th Battalion is attacking with us and we'll be helped by a British barrage, so it shouldn't be too bad.'

Tom looked over the shell-torn wasteland before him. He could not see the Germans but he knew they were there, and he resolved to fight them as bravely as he could. He felt no sense of excitement or adventure in war now, but he did not want to let his mates down, or fail in his duty.

At dusk the British artillery intensified its bombardment, and the German artillery, warned by this that an attack was imminent, began to reply. Hundreds of shells, some of them British shells falling short, began to land among the men of the 3rd Battalion, and soon wounded men in dozens were crying for the stretcher-bearers.

The moment for the attack came. Paddy leapt forward, running from shellhole to shellhole for cover. The others followed, but soon a German starshell burst above them, lighting up the scene like day, and immediately the clatter of the machine-guns broke from the German front. Next the German artillery concentrated on the attackers, and as Tom watched, his comrades began to fall in great heaps, sometimes ten or twenty in an instant. Not far from Tom, George Watts collapsed, almost cut in half by a burst of machine-gun fire. Paddy Halliday was shot in the shoulder, and Joe Thompson's rifle was smashed

from his hand by a piece of shrapnel. Where minutes before two or three hundred men had begun to advance, now only thirty or forty could still move forward.

It seemed impossible to go on, and Tom dived into a large shellhole. Paddy was already there, nursing a second wound in his leg. In a moment Rodney followed them, then Joe and Jack. No other Australians could be seen. Around Tom the roaring shells threw up great fountains of earth, the machine-gun bullets hummed angrily, and all was desolation.

'The Germans are coming!' Jack cried, and from the darkness loomed the square helmets of the enemy. The Australians opened fire: some Germans fell, and the rest dived into shellholes.

'We'll bomb them out,' said Paddy, as he grasped some grenades and painfully raised himself onto his wounded leg. 'Is everyone ready?'

Suddenly there was a brilliant flash. Tom felt himself floating softly through the air, then he was slammed against the wall of the shellhole. A small shell had exploded close by, and Tom was bruised, dizzy and deafened. Beside him Paddy Halliday lay face down. A large slab of shell had smashed into his back, and he was dead. On the edge of the crater Jack Sloane was groaning: he had been blown clean out of the shellhole, and was shot through the shoulder with a piece of shell. Not far away Joe Thompson lay wounded in the side, and he was passing bombs up to Rodney, who was crouched just below the rim of the crater, hurling them into the darkness beyond.

Tom realized that Rodney was alone, bombing back the attacking Germans. Feebly he searched for a rifle, and as he found one a figure rose from the darkness and aimed a revolver at Rodney. Tom fired, and a German officer tumbled into the shellhole. Another German ran forward, bayonet raised. Tom fired again, and the German dropped his rifle and staggered back. Through the bursts of shellfire and the pale flame of Rodney's bombs Tom could see more Germans trying to advance, but Rodney sat by the edge of the crater, hurling bombs at any who attempted to come forward.

There came a lull in the fighting.

'We're nearly out of bombs, cobber,' Joe warned Rodney.

Rodney looked around. 'We'll have to get back,' he said. 'I can't see anyone else alive, and I don't want to fight the whole German Army by myself. Tom, can you hear me? We'll have to retreat. I'll carry Joe, if you look after Jack. Do you think you can manage it?' Tom nodded weakly. 'Right, off you go. I'll cover you, then follow.'

So the little party withdrew, struggling back, until at last they met some stretcher-bearers. 'Here mate, hold onto my belt,' a bearer told Tom. 'We'll get you out all right.'

Dazed and dizzy from the shellburst, Tom did as he was told. His brain whirled as he walked: now he saw the shattered earth, now his hands on the stretcher-bearer's belt, now the shambling wounded around him, now the great red flashes of the bursting shells. The night seemed endless as he lurched along, but at last the stretcher-bearer turned and said, 'All right mate, lie down here and get some rest.'

Tom realized vaguely that the terrible shells had become only a distant rumble; he sank down thankfully, and in a few moments was fast asleep.

Two days later Tom watched his battalion come out of the

Equipment used by the Australians: right: a hand grenade, called a Mills Bomb Mark 5; far right: gunners wearing gas masks; below: on Pozières ridge, a trench mortar being loaded with a shell called a 'flying pig'.

line. A pitifully small group of men marched by, less than a hundred of the nine hundred who had charged so dashingly only four weeks before. Every face reflected the horror of the men's recent experiences. They shuffled past, looking neither right nor left, heeding nothing, careless even that they had escaped from death. They were the survivors, the lucky few. And Rodney, who had defended the shell crater so bravely, and who had saved so many of his comrades, was not among them.

Twenty-three thousand Australian soldiers were killed or wounded at Pozières. This was about 60 per cent of the entire A.I.F. in France, and about one two-hundredth of the population of Australia. Never had so many Australians been made casualties in one battle, and never had a battle such severe effects upon the morale of survivors. This battle, more than any other, changed the outlook of the men of the A.I.F. Whereas before it had still been possible to think of war as exciting or glorious, now it was only possible to keep on fighting by being grimly determined to do one's duty. Before Pozières most soldiers thought they would probably survive the war; after it many thought they would probably die. From then on they began to think in ways utterly different from civilians in Australia, and to behave not as citizens serving temporarily in a wartime army, but as soldiers condemned till the end of their days to an eternal round of fighting, pain and death.

8 The 1916–17 winter

Slowly men recovered from the ordeal of Pozières. Reinforcements came from Australia, and the Australian divisions were given rest in quiet sectors of the front. Tom got over his shell shock, and became a sergeant. In October Mick Sloane rejoined the battalion, as a corporal in Tom's platoon.

In November the Australians began a fresh ordeal – winter. The 1916–17 winter was the harshest in France for forty years. In November and December incessant rain made the entire battle area a bog, and for months men could not move without wading through deep, sticky slush. A few were drowned in the quagmire. Others were stuck fast and crouched helpless under the German guns until they died or were rescued. Even a short journey required great effort, and large numbers of soldiers collapsed from sheer exhaustion.

In the front line conditions were miserable beyond description. The garrison had to stand knee deep in mud, sleepless, wet, shivering, and often with little to eat or drink because rations could not reach them. Sickness spread, and hundreds of men were evacuated with 'trench feet', an affliction which caused feet immersed in water for a long time to swell and split painfully, making it impossible for soldiers to walk. Orders were given that every man had to change into dry socks each day, and also rub his feet with whale oil, specially issued as a cure. But often in the front line these things were impossible,

Mud in the trenches, France, winter 1916 . . . and winter 1917.

On the Flanders front, 1917.

and while the rain and mud remained, 'trench feet' was a serious problem for the army.

In December snow fell and froze the ground. The horrors of the mud disappeared, but the cold in the trenches was so bitter that sometimes the troops of both sides stamped about in the open, ignoring the war in an effort to keep warm.

Yet the normal routine of war continued. Generally, a battalion would garrison the front for a 'tour' of about eight days. About half a battalion would actually occupy the front, so that each soldier was in the line for three or four days. The other half of the battalion would man support trenches and provide work parties, which every night carried rations or ammunition up to the line, or dug trenches, or strengthened the wire in No Man's Land, or laid wooden duckboards across the mud.

When a battalion had completed its 'tour' of duty, it would be relieved by another battalion, and go into a camp a mile or two behind the line. When every battalion in a division had completed its 'tour' the division was withdrawn, and usually sent far behind the lines into a permanent camp with huts, a canteen, a training ground, and perhaps some entertainment facilities. Those due for leave in England were called out; an Australian soldier got ten days' English leave about every ten

A billet behind the line, winter 1916.

37

above: *An* estaminet *near the front line, 1916.*

below: *Soldiers in a dugout behind the line, winter 1917.*

months, depending on when his turn came. The others would repair their weapons, mend their kit, and make good any equipment deficiencies from the battalion store. Subsequent days were spent drilling or training. At nights men might draw some of their pay and wander across to the nearest *estaminet*, or small restaurant, where the cheerful French proprietress would serve them eggs and chips and big bottles of red or white wine. After tea the soldiers would sit around the fire and chat, or make the rafters ring with their favourite wartime songs, 'Mademoiselle from Armentières', 'Australia will be there', 'It's a long way to Tipperary', and many others, until the military police came to check on the men, and the soldiers absent without leave dived through the back door to avoid being arrested.

Then one evening the battalion would form up, and march back to the line and the guns.

In February 1917 Tom and about twenty others of the 3rd Battalion were warned that they were to raid the German trenches near Gueudecourt. They were shown a model of their objective, and for two weeks they practised their attack. Each man had a special job – capturing prisoners, blowing up dugouts, protecting the flanks, and so on – and each man carried only the weapons necessary for his own particular job. This was very different from a battle, when men carried not only their weapons and rations, but also an entrenching tool, and perhaps a pick or a shovel, or mortar bombs, or machine-gun ammunition, or barbed wire, or some other necessary piece of equipment.

One night, when all was ready, the raiders filed into the front line. Down came the British barrage, the attack whistles blew, and the men scrambled into No Man's Land. Already green and red lights were curling up from the German lines as the enemy's infantry called on their artillery to help them.

Tom was about halfway across No Man's Land when he felt a sharp pain in his chest, and fell down. He had been hit by a

above: *Dugouts near Messines, winter 1917.*

right: *3rd Battalion men waiting to advance, 1917.*

Stretcher-bearers carrying a wounded man to the rear, France, winter 1916.

right: Australian wounded waiting for ambulances, and then in a dressing station, France, 1917.

machine-gun bullet, and the wound seemed serious. Tom lay quietly, trying to staunch the blood, waiting for help. Ahead he could hear shouts and explosions as the Australians jumped into the German trench, and soon he could pick out men running back towards him. A German went past, hands on his head, and behind him came an Australian waving his bayonet dangerously to make sure his prisoner kept moving.

'Australia!' Tom called.

The Australian stopped. 'Who's that?'

Tom recognized Mick Sloane's voice. 'It's Tom Mitchell, Mick. Give us a hand will you? I'm shot in the chest.'

'Crikey!' said Mick. 'Here Fritz, grab hold of my mate. And be careful or I'll skewer you!'

The German did not understand English but he followed Mick's meaning clearly enough, and obediently he bent down and lifted Tom onto his shoulder while Mick led the way back to the Australian trench. There two stretcher-bearers put a field dressing on Tom's wound, and bore him quickly along the deep communication trenches to the rear. Soon Tom was at the regimental aid post. His wound was cleaned and dressed, and

then other stretcher-bearers carried him to the roadhead to put him on a truck which drove him to a big casualty clearing station well behind the line.

Tom was very lucky. Had there been a big battle with many wounded, or had the clutching mud made stretcher-bearing difficult, he may have taken hours, even days, to reach the casualty clearing station, and he may even have died while he waited. As it was, a doctor was soon probing his wound, and before morning Tom was marked for an operation in Blighty.

'Blighty' was the name soldiers gave England, and it also meant a wound serious enough to need treatment in England. Soldiers who received a 'Blighty' wound escaped from the war for a while, so Tom was very pleased. He was taken first to a large hospital near the French coast, then across the Channel to Dover, and finally to a warm bed in an Australian hospital in London. It was only five days since he had been shot.

9 The war ends

Outside A.I.F. Headquarters in Horseferry Road, London.

below: *Inside the Anzac Buffet, Victoria Street, London.*

Tom's wound healed slowly. He was in hospital or convalescing for over a year. After several months he was able to go exploring around London, and often he would call at A.I.F. Headquarters in Horseferry Road for his mail and a cheap meal. Then he would visit some of London's famous buildings, or poke into quiet corners, or see a theatre matinée or a play.

News of the A.I.F. came regularly. In the Middle East the Light Horse was part of the Allied force which was advancing from Egypt across the Sinai Desert, and they had pushed deep into Palestine, driving the Turks before them. In France the Australians had fought in several big battles: at Bullecourt in April and May 1917, in June at Messines, and from September to November in the Passchendaele area, in Belgium. In March 1918 a great German offensive pushed back the Allied armies, and a little later Tom heard of fresh glory the A.I.F. had won in helping to stem the German tide – at Hazebrouck, at Dernancourt, at Morlancourt, and especially at Villers-Bretonneux. By now the Australians were seasoned soldiers, skilled in war, and considered by friend and foe as among the best troops in all the Allied armies.

Tom returned to the front in April 1918, and found the First Division at Hazebrouck. The other four Australian divisions were farther south, on the Somme, but everywhere the German advance had been stopped, and the Australian and New Zealand infantry were beginning a new activity, called 'peaceful penetration'.

Between May and July 1918 small groups of Australians, sometimes one, sometimes twenty, would climb from their trenches, creep through the tall summer crops in No Man's Land, and fall suddenly upon a German post or trench, killing, wounding and capturing. This was called 'peaceful penetration', and alone of all the armies the Anzacs waged it regularly. They terrorized their enemies, and at least once at this time German soldiers refused to enter the line when they learnt that their opponents would be Australians.

Lieutenant-General Sir John Monash, Commander of the Australian Corps from 31 May 1918 until after the Armistice.

left: *The desolate battlefield of Passchendaele.*

In time, the Australians by 'peaceful penetration' captured hundreds of prisoners, many trenches, several miles of ground, and even a town (Merris). They gained more by this method than they had won in all the great battles of 1916 and 1917, and for a fraction of the cost in Australian lives.

One warm summer's day, not long after Tom had rejoined the battalion, Mick Sloane crept out into No Man's Land. Soon he returned and whispered, 'Hey you blokes! I've found a German machine-gun post! About six Germans. Get some bombs and we'll go across and grab 'em.'

Tom, Jack and Joe collected their weapons, and followed Mick quietly through the long grass into No Man's Land. Soon they heard coughs and the click of weapons from the post ahead, and stealthily they spread out to surround the Germans. When everyone was ready Mick and Joe hurled their bombs, and as they exploded Tom and Jack bounded forward with rifle and bayonet.

The bombs exploded fairly in the enemy post. Three Germans were killed, one was wounded, and the two remaining lay dazed by the explosions.

'Right Fritz,' Tom told them. 'Pick up your mate, and let's get moving.' The Germans lifted their wounded comrade, Jack hoisted the machine-gun onto his shoulder, and in a moment the whole party was moving rapidly back to the Australian line. Everyone arrived safely, and as Joe escorted the prisoners to the rear Mick exclaimed jubilantly, 'Well, that's not a bad way to put in an afternoon! We must do it again!'

'Peaceful penetration' showed that German morale was not nearly so high as in former years, and by August 1918 the Allied generals had planned a big attack on the enemy's defences along the valley of the Somme. Its spearhead was to be the newly formed Australian Corps, of five divisions under an Australian leader, General Monash, and the Canadian Corps, of four divisions. They would be supported by British troops to the north, and French troops to the south. The attackers would use many new devices of war – planes, tanks and co-ordinated artillery barrages – and everything was arranged carefully and secretly, so that the Germans would have no warning of the approaching assault.

The attack was made on 8 August 1918. Before dawn on that

Australians before the 'August 8' battle, 1918.

day, the shells of 2,000 guns crashed down upon the German positions. At the same time 456 tanks lumbered ahead of the Allied infantry who rose and advanced quickly through the morning fog, brushing aside the dazed defenders. The Australians and Canadians were especially successful, and rounded up thousands of prisoners. The German line was pushed back several kilometres, and the German generals were convinced that they must try to end the war.

After this great victory the Allied armies began to advance all along the Western Front. Steadily their successes multiplied until it was plain that Germany would be defeated. The Australian infantry took part in much heavy fighting, but they pushed forward tirelessly, sometimes by planned attack, sometimes by 'peaceful penetration'. They captured the valley of the Somme, where so many had died since 1915, they overran the great fortress system of Mont St Quentin, they broke through the strong defences of the famous Hindenburg Line. They

advanced almost 65 kilometres (40 miles), and by their deeds they greatly assisted the victory of the Allies (see map on p. 31).

(see map on p. 31)

But by the end of the war the soldiers of the A.I.F. were exhausted. In the last months they had fought continuously, many had lost two or three stone in weight, and some were so weary that they fell asleep as they marched. Their clothes were in rags, and they moved with the jerky mannerisms and fixed stares of men who had been pushed to the limits of their endurance. Battalions of a thousand men had been reduced by sickness and battle to fewer than a hundred; several battalions had been disbanded, and none could muster more than 300 men. That gay self-confidence which had marked Australians in the days before the landing at Gallipoli had utterly vanished, and was never to appear again. Yet always the Australians took

right: *Australians advancing, 23 August 1918.*

below right: *Soldiers before the attack on Mont St Quentin.*

below: *The other nationalities of infantry soldiers who fought on the Western Front: American, British, French and German.*

their objectives, fighting on despite every hardship. They remained loyal to the mates who had shared with them the risks of battle, and to their country.

On 21 September 1918 the 3rd Battalion made a small attack beyond the village of Hargicourt. There a German artillery shell killed Jack Sloane, who had landed at Anzac so long before, and now was struck down at the last. After this fight the 3rd Battalion was withdrawn to rest, and a few weeks later, on 11 November 1918, as the soldiers were preparing to return to the line, word came that the war was over.

Victory! After four long, bitter years. A surge of relief passed through Tom. He did not sing or dance as the civilians did; he was too weary for that. Yet gladly he realized that he would live, and get home to Australia again, and gratefully he thanked his good fortune.

But other thoughts crowded upon him. The A.I.F., which had won such fame and such glory, must now disband. The 3rd Battalion, which for so long had been home to him, would soon be no more. And Tom thought of his mates – of Lieutenant Ross dead on distant Anzac; of Andy Ellis lying where he had fallen at the Bloody Angle; of Paddy and Rodney killed at Pozières; of Jack, struck down in the last days of the war; and of many other good friends resting forever far from their country. As he realized that shortly he must leave these old comrades, Tom felt the great wrench of parting. There came upon him a sense of all the horror and futility of war, with its pain and its suffering, its slaughter and its sacrifice, and the way it brought so many ordinary men, men such as you see every day in the street, to misery and death.

10 The world after 1918

Almost all the countries of Europe suffered as a result of the Great War. Millions of soldiers died, and millions of other people endured hunger and privation. The First World War was the most terrible of all the wars which man had fought to that time.

The map of Europe was changed dramatically by the war. Look again at the maps at the beginning of the book showing how the war altered the boundaries of the European nations. Germany, Austria–Hungary, Russia and Turkey all lost territory, France gained territory, and particularly in eastern Europe many new nations were formed. Most of the countries defeated in the war overthrew their old rulers and introduced new forms of government.

There were great changes outside Europe too. Germany lost all her colonies; the United States became more important and her president proposed the League of Nations to work towards future world peace; in Asia, Japan became more powerful; and all over the world people began to wonder whether empires were a good thing, and some colonies began to seek greater independence from their mother countries.

There were technical advances: for example, the demands of war accelerated the development of aircraft, the wireless, the means of mass production, and medical, surgical and chemical knowledge.

Perhaps the most important changes were in people's attitudes. The war allowed women to become more prominent in the workforce and in public life, and to a degree it increased the importance of the ordinary man and woman in politics and society. Above all, it produced a great disillusionment with war itself: after 1918 people could no longer consider war a glorious and admirable way of settling disputes, and they hoped that the First World War would be 'the war to end all wars'.

How did things change in Australia after the war?

Of 330,000 Australians who sailed with the A.I.F. to fight, about two-thirds were killed or wounded during the war. A total of 63,000 men, roughly one in every seventy of the entire population of Australia, were killed. About 150,000 were wounded, and 2,000 of these were to spend the rest of their lives in hospital. If you had enlisted in 1914, as Tom did, probably you would have been killed, and almost certainly you would have been wounded at least once.

Almost certainly also, your entire outlook would have been changed by the Great War. Before 1914 you would have felt proud of the British Empire, and you would have looked on war as a glorious and exciting adventure, something which all real men should be glad to take part in. After 1918 you would still support the Empire, and you would be proud of Australia's great achievements during the war, but you would be completely disillusioned with war, regarding it as something to be avoided wherever possible.

You would also have A.I.F. friends and memories which would tend to cut you off from those who had not fought in the war. You would have risked your life in terrible battles which others could only read about, and so necessarily some of your values and attitudes would differ from theirs. For example, they would want to forget the war now that it was over; but you would not be able to, because your experiences had been too prolonged and too terrible. They would want returned soldiers to behave like civilians again; but you would find this difficult, because you had been so long a soldier.

This is what happened to Tom and his friends. A division of opinion arose in Australian society, which was confirmed by the Second World War, and which continues to this very day. Today many who have fought in war want Australia to continue celebrating Anzac Day, while more and more the ones who have not fought, do not. I do not know what you think of Anzac Day. You may approve of it, or you may disapprove of it. But I hope that Tom's story will at least help you understand what Anzac stands for, and why some Australians still remember the First World War.